good luck

summersdale

To:

From:

Summersdale Publishers Ltd
46 West Street
Chichester
West Sussex
PO19 1RP
UK

www.summersdale.com

Printed and bound by Tien Wah Press, Singapore

ISBN: 978-1-84024-765-7

Substantial discounts on bulk quantities of Summersdale books are available to
corporations, professional associations and other organisations. For details telephone
Summersdale Publishers on (+44-1243-771107), fax (+44-1243-786300) or email
(nicky@summersdale.com).

good luck

Poppy Bell

Here's wishing you
all the best…

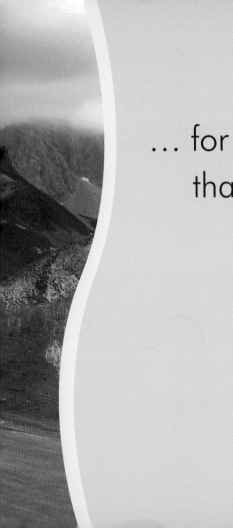

... for the challenges
that lie ahead.

You might need some
reassurance…

... or a friendly hug to give you courage.

Luck comes in
many forms.

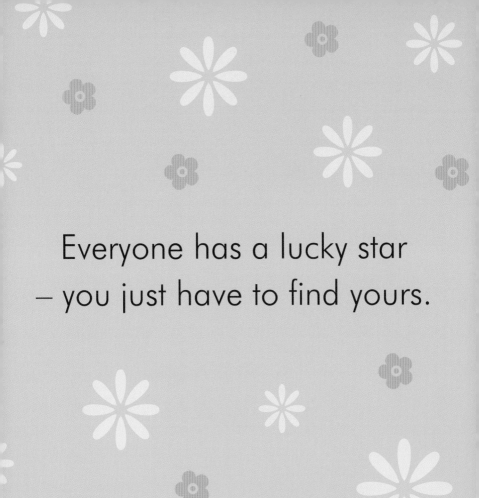

Everyone has a lucky star
– you just have to find yours.

Sometimes you just have to look in the right places.

A lucky charm…

... can bring confidence.

It's not just about getting the best cards — you have to play them right.

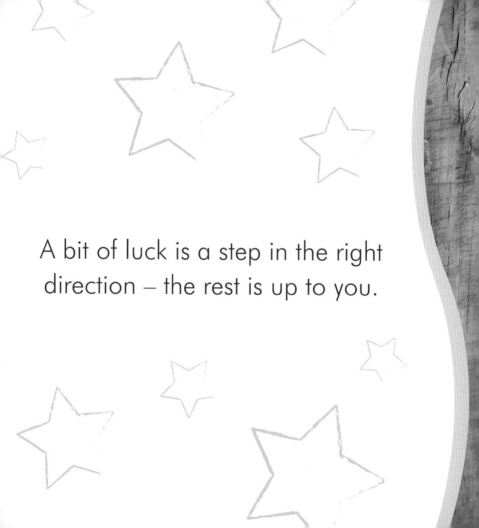

A bit of luck is a step in the right direction – the rest is up to you.

So find a calm
state of mind...

… and put your
thoughts in order.

Take things one
step at a time.

Positive thoughts pave
the way to success.

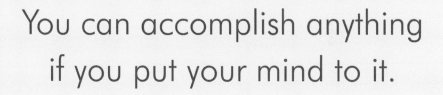

You can accomplish anything
if you put your mind to it.

Set your sights on your goal.

Don't be distracted
by the competition.

When the going gets tough, remember to take a break.

You've got a lot
to learn…

... and if you're not
successful first time...

... remember that every cloud has a silver lining.

Don't panic if
you get stuck.

Try a new approach
– be inventive!

Let hope burn bright
in your heart.

Keep reaching
for the sun.

Remember to take care
of the little details...

… and to see the bigger picture too.

Sometimes you need to take a leap of faith.

Make a wish and believe
that it can come true.

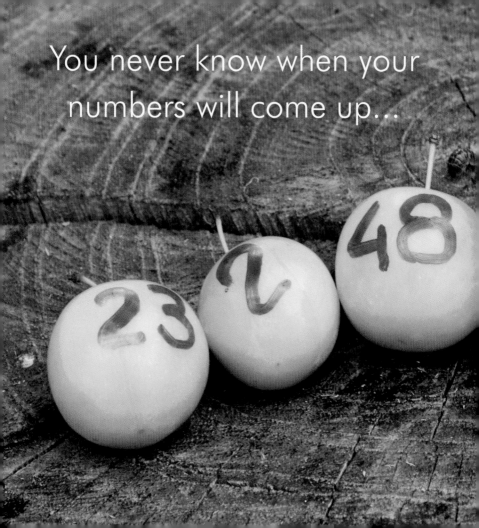

... so take a chance.

Your friends are there
to hold your hand...

... and to chill out with
when it all gets too much.

Thoughts and prayers
of others can carry
you a long way.

You never know what
fate will bring you.

Rejoice in your successes
along the way…

… and celebrate them
with your pals.

Cherish every unexpected
treasure that you find.

A beautiful dream
is worth pursuing.

So what are you waiting for? Go for it!

I'll be crossing my
fingers for you.

Good luck!

PHOTO CREDITS

Have you enjoyed this book? If so, why not write a
review on your favourite website?

Thanks very much for buying this Summersdale book.

www.summersdale.com